An Illustrated Memory

Based on a true story

G. Deeya
Art by: Valentina Esposito

Copyright © 2021 by G. Deeya

Written by: G. Deeya
Art by: Valentina Esposito
Layout and Edits by: Hope Boyd

All rights reserved. This book or any portion thereof may not be reproduced or used in any manner whatsoever without the express written permission of the publisher except for the use of brief quotations in a book review or scholarly journal.

First Printing: 2021
ISBN 978-1-7342370-3-0
Library of Congress Control Number: 2021914326

Grace Ekwue
752 N Main St #154
Mansfield, TX 76063-3203

G. Deeya is a Nigerian-American poet, educator, and author.
G. Deeya is Grace Ekwue's pen name.

"Dee ya" [deh-YAH] means "write it down" in Igbo (a Nigerian language). Phonetically, G. Deeya sounds like "jide ya" [gee-DEH-yah], which means "hold onto it" in Igbo.

"I wanted to write down and preserve my spoken word pieces so that they can be held and carry on."

G. Deeya was born in Nigeria, raised on the East Coast, and spent most of her life in her current state of Texas. As a former U.S. History teacher, she made time to incorporate poetry and children's books in the classroom. She has written and directed student plays and poetry showcases. When the curtains closed, her desire to preserve her writings sprung forth.

It was during this time that G. Deeya ventured into writing children's books. She carefully weaves wordplay and vivid imagery that shines through in her poems and books.

When she is not writing, G. Deeya enjoys all the fine arts and culture that the world has to offer.

For Ma:

Who treasured
all of our performances
and accomplishments,
both great and small.

Snorkeler #9.
No official name.
She was a 5th grade extra.
A small role
in the school Christmas play.

But Hope was content.
Ready to perform
alongside the big names:
Santa. Rudolph. Mrs. Claus...

But then,
minutes before showtime,
She peeked out
behind the curtain
and into the crowd.

She saw Mom.

Working long hours
at the restaurant,
used to taking orders and tips.

But tonight,
Mom ordered her steps
and tip-toed
through packed aisles
to see her daughter perform.

Still dressed in uniform,
she was ready to cheer
for Snorkeler #9.

But Hope didn't want to disappoint.
Mom sacrificed rest for
elementary entertainment.

No.
Mom deserved more than extra. Hope wasn't going to stay underwater tonight.

She looked over at Ms. Red,
her music teacher,
unapologetic,
ready to get on stage
and make this show epic.

Her goal wasn't to upstage...
just complement
each performance.

Cue curtains.
Cue lights.
Cue music.

Glance at Mom.
Smile.
Wave.
Perform!

and became the unexpected harmony on every song.

The extra elf...

Santa's sidekick...

Rudolph's best friend...

and, of course, Snorkeler #9.

After curtain call and final bows, Hope ran up as Mom said, "Wow! Great job, Hopie! I didn't know you had so many parts!"

"I'm just glad it was worth your time, Ma!", she replied.

If only Ms. Red could understand...

But in her eyes, Hope went too far.

Things got out of hand and didn't go as planned.

If she only knew
that Hope was only trying
to match Mom's sacrifice,
striving to repay her
with the gift of time.
Would that have
changed her mind?

CLAP CLAP CLAP

Because Mom came to the play...
And she deserved more than Snorkeler #9.

Also by G. Deeya:

"Hear Us"

www.ingramcontent.com/pod-product-compliance
Lightning Source LLC
Chambersburg PA
CBHW041820040426
42452CB00004B/160